ROSEMARY STANTON

EASY DIET COOKBOOK

THE Low-fat way

KÖNEMANN

Low-fat Eating

Losing weight is not complicated. The first step is knowing how much fat there is in everyday foods. If you want to lose weight, you should aim to eat no more than 30–40 grams of fat a day. Eat more delicious fibre-rich foods and you won't go hungry.

What makes people fat?

For many years, nutritionists have taught that too much of almost any kind of food could be converted to body fat. Recent research has shown this to be wrong: in almost all cases, the only thing that adds to body fat is the fat we eat.

It seems the body does not like turning protein into fat, and will only convert carbohydrates into body fat if you eat huge amounts. Carbohydrates are generally used to power the body. Any excess is stored as glycogen in the muscles, and can also increase the energy used for metabolism. It's not until you eat more than 500 grams of carbohydrate at one sitting—the amount in more than 30 slices of bread—that the body converts it to fat. This means we should stop avoiding bread and blame the spread instead.

Alcohol, so often blamed for excess fat, is not directly converted to body fat. It's obvious, since alcoholics who take in many calories from alcohol but eat little food are almost always thin. Alcohol, however, does contribute indirectly to body fat by making it more difficult for the body to burn up the fats in food. Alcohol plus fat is therefore a bad combination for those who gain weight easily.

Sugar (a rapidly absorbed carbohydrate) when combined with fat may have a similar effect in preventing the body burning fat to provide energy. But in all cases, it's fatty foods that are the root cause of excess weight.

Why people are getting fatter

In Western countries, the food supply contains increasing amounts of hidden fats. In years past, you could see fat slathered over the weekend roast and notice that the roast potatoes soaked it up. You could also see the fat on the edge of chops and the slabs of butter that went on to bread. Nowadays we are less aware of the fats in the food supply, and some fats have managed to create such a good impression for themselves that many people are unaware of their true nature. Margarine, for example, is more than 80 per cent fat—the same high percentage as butter—yet most people think of it as being somehow less fatty.

Snack foods and fast foods are great contributors to fat intake. Who would have guessed that a modern-day hamburger has around 30 grams of fat, compared with 18 grams in the old-fashioned variety? And how many people know that the smaller the French fries, the greater their fat content? And did you know that the average Australian now buys four meals a week away from home, many of them fatty fast foods?

Even though more people cut the fat off their meat and there are reduced-fat dairy products, low-fat dressings and mayonnaises, and fat-reduced pies, spreads and ice-creams, we are still eating a lot of fat. Most people don't realise it—many buy fat-reduced products and then eat twice as much of them!

All kinds of fat make you fat, although some are otherwise quite beneficial. The fats in avocado, olive oil, fish, nuts and seeds are very good for you, but they are just as fattening as other harmful fats.

Exercise, or rather the lack of it, also has a lot to do with body fat. Most people spend so much time sitting in cars, at a desk or watching television that they have little time to be physically active. When people walked more, had more

Vegetables and grains make deliciously filling low-fat meals.

FOODS WITH NO FAT	
Food	**Fat (grams)**
All fruits, except avocado	0
All vegetables	0
Skim milk	0
Non-fat yoghurt	0
Honey and sugar	0
Soft drinks	0
Beer, wine, other alcoholic drinks	0
Herbs and spices	0

FOODS WITH A LOW FAT CONTENT	
Food	**Fat (grams)**
Baked beans ,1 cup	1
Beans, 1 cup (eg kidney)	1
Bread, 2 slices, any kind	1
Breakfast cereals (except toasted muesli), av. bowl	1
Couscous, 1 cup	1
Crumpets, 2	1
Muffin, 2 halves	1
Pasta, wholemeal, cooked, 1 cup (150 g)	1
Raisin bread, 1 slice	1
Rice, cooked, 2 cups	1
Spaghetti, cooked, 2 cups	1

OTHER FOODS	
Food	**Fat (grams)**
Apple pie, home-made, av. serve	28
Avocado, 1/2	20
Bacon, 1 rasher	10
Bacon & eggs	32
Bagel, 1	2
Biscuits, sweet, each	4
Biscuits, savoury crackers, each	1
Butter, 20 g	16
Caesar salad, av. serve	30
Cake, black forest, av. slice	34
Cake, carrot, av. slice	42
Cake, sponge with cream, av. slice	23
Cheese, 30 g	10
Cheesecake, homemade, av. slice	55
Chicken, fried, each piece	14
Chicken breast, no skin, av. serve	5
Chiko roll, 1	17
Chocolate, 100 g	27
Coconut milk, canned, 1/2 cup	16
Crispbread, 3	1
Croissant, 1	17

OTHER FOODS

Food	Fat (grams)
Dressing, salad, av. serve	10
Cream-based pasta sauce, 1/2 cup	45
Egg, 1	6
Fish, av. piece, grilled	2
Fish, battered, av. piece	24
Hamburger, fast food, 1	30
Ice-cream, 100 ml serve	5
Ice-cream, rich, 2 scoops	15
Ice-cream, choc-coated heart, 1	21
Lamb, lean steak, 100 g	5
Lamb chops, grilled, 2	24
Lasagne, av. serve	23
Margarine, 20 g	16
Mayonnaise, 1 tablespoon	18
Meat pie, 1	24
Milk, fat-reduced, 250 ml	3
Milk, regular, 250 ml	10
Muffin, 2 halves	1
Muffin, cake type, 1	8
Nuts, 50 g	28
Oil, all kinds, 1 tablespoon	20
Pastry, Danish, 1	15
Peanut butter, 20 g	10
Pecan pie, av. serve	33
Pizza, 1/2 large	18
Pork, lean only, 100 g	5
Pork chop, 1	30
Potato chips, hot, av. serve	21
Potato crisps, 50 g packet	16
Quiche, homemade, av. serve	44
Salami, 50 g	19
Sausage, grilled 1	15
Schnitzel, av. serve	27
Spaghetti, homemade tomato sauce, av. serve	2
Spaghetti meat sauce, av. serve	18
Steak, grilled, av. serve	33
Steak, trimmed, av. serve	10
Toasted muesli, av. serve	9
Tofu, steamed, 100 g	4
Turkey, 100 g	2
Yoghurt, 200 g	9

Rosemary Stanton's Fat and Fibre Counter (available from bookshops and some newsagents) lists the fat content in more than 1500 commonly eaten foods.

active jobs and had more active leisure time, most stayed slim.

The pursuit of excellence in sport has also meant that fewer people *play* sport. Many who aren't champions think they should watch rather than play. Children, in particular, feel foolish if they don't excel at sport, and many stop playing sport early.

Losing body fat

To lose body fat, you need to cut back on the fat you eat and exercise a bit more. That's about all most people need to do.

The old idea of counting calories has unimpressive results. Most people who start off counting calories give up and regain any weight they have lost. Also, as we mentioned, calories from fats are more likely to make you fat than those from protein, carbohydrate and alcohol. So it's useless, as well as boring, to pore over calorie charts.

However, it's not useless to take a look at how much fat you're eating and find out which foods have little or no fat.

10 tips for low-fat shopping

1. Fill your trolley with fruit and vegetables first.
2. Buy low-fat milk and yoghurt, cottage cheese, and low-fat (less than 7 per cent) hard cheeses.
3. Don't buy spreads—if you don't have them, you can't use them.
4. Spend more time in the supermarket aisle with the pasta, rice, couscous or other grains, and pass by the biscuits and confectionery.
5. Buy tuna and other canned fish in water or brine rather than in oil.
6. Plan meals around vegetables and let the meat fit in around them.
7. Buy lots of interesting breads: rolls, flatbreads and fresh loaves in different shapes.
8. Buy raisin bread instead of biscuits or cakes (even cracker biscuits are high in fat).
9. If you need pastry, buy filo and brush with the minimum of oil.
10. Read the label: many manufacturers now say how much fat is in foods. Ingredients must be listed according to the proportion in which they are used. If any type of fat is near the top of the list, beware. If fat or oil is well down the list, the quantity is probably not worth worrying about.

How much fat?

There's no need to aim for no-fat eating: that would make your diet quite inadequate, and also lacking in flavour. If you need to lose weight, aim to eat 30–40 grams of fat a day. The lower figure is appropriate for women and short men, the higher one for the average male and very tall women.

Although we can't be definite about the rate at which anyone will lose body fat, a loss of 1–2 kilograms a month is excellent. If you think that's not much, consider what a 500 g tub of margarine looks like—that's half a kilo of fat. Losing the equivalent of 2–4 tubs of fat a month is quite an achievement. With regular low-fat eating, body fat losses are also more likely to be permanent.

Low-fat eating also means avoiding hunger. Most foods either have a lot of fat and little fibre, or a lot of fibre and little fat (nuts are the major exception, as they have lots of both). Eating foods with less fat will give you more fibre, and fibre is filling.

People who have tried many diets often say that they break their diet through boredom, and because they are always hungry. The wide variety of delicious, low-fat, filling foods available makes it easier to stick to this healthful way of eating until it becomes a way of life. Your dinner plate can be heaped with vegetables, hearty helpings of rice, pasta or potatoes, and a smaller portion of meat. You won't go hungry because you'll be eating more. And once you explore the vast array of fruits and vegetables, cereals, breads, grains, legumes and seafoods around, you certainly won't be bored.

The recipes in this book will help. The soups have an average of 3.5 grams of fat per serve; the salads and vegetables have an average of 4 grams of fat; the dishes in the pasta, rice and grain section average only 5 grams each per serve, the main courses come in at an average of 6 grams of fat, and the desserts are all entirely fat-free.

Combining fruits, vegetables, breads, cereals, low-fat dairy products, and some seafoods, chicken or lean meat will give you the basis of good low-fat eating. And remember to use plenty of herbs and spices for flavour.

The low-fat party

Lots of low-fat foods can be served at parties and special occasions:
❖ Crisp vegetables with a dip blended from cooked chickpeas, lemon juice and garlic.
❖ The flesh of a roasted eggplant blended with lemon juice and roasted cumin powder. Serve with flatbread crisped in a slow oven.
❖ Seafoods, but not battered or crumbed. Oysters, prawns, scallops, crab, yabbies and fish of all varieties are low in fat. Choose a Thai-style chilli sauce for dipping, or use lime or lemon juice, or low-fat yoghurt with fresh herbs and lemon juice.
❖ Skinned chicken breasts marinated in lime juice, garlic, chilli, lemon grass, ginger and a spoonful of palm sugar; grill or barbecue.
❖ Un-dressed salads; serve olive oil and balsamic vinegar separately.

SUGGESTED MENU

Food	Fat (grams)
Milk in tea and coffee during the day	5
Breakfast	
Fresh fruit	0
Breakfast cereal	1
Milk on cereal, reduced fat	3
Toast	1
Marmalade	0
Morning tea	
Piece of raisin bread	1
Lunch	
Pasta salad (see recipe)	6
Crusty bread (no butter or margarine)	1
Low-fat yoghurt, 200g	0
Fresh fruit salad	0
Afternoon tea	
Apple	0
Dinner	
Lamb with red capsicum sauce (see recipe)	7
Steamed new potatoes	0
Green salad	0
1 teaspoon olive oil + herbs & lemon on salad	5
Sweet vanilla peaches (see recipe page 56)	0
Total fat for the day	**30**

❖ Vegetables—fresh asparagus, cherry tomatoes, green beans, roasted capsicum; leeks (marinate in lemon juice, fry in a non-stick pan); steamed tiny new potatoes, tossed with fresh dill; barbecued zucchini sprinkled with balsamic vinegar; steamed pumpkin balls.
❖ A large bowl or platter of fruits for dessert or with drinks.

Fresh vegetables make colourful party platters

Soups

The recipes in this section all contain very little fat, so you can eat them as often as you like. Add some bread (2 slices contain 1 gram of fat) and fresh fruit (no fat) and you have a filling, low-fat meal.

Sweet Potato, Pumpkin and Orange Soup

Preparation time: 30 minutes
Total cooking time: 20 minutes
Serves 4

1 onion, chopped
1 clove garlic, crushed
1 sprig fresh rosemary
750 g peeled and seeded pumpkin chunks
500 g orange sweet potato, peeled and cut into chunks
3 cups chicken stock
1 cup orange juice

1. Combine all ingredients in a large pan; bring to the boil, cover and simmer for 15–20 minutes, or until vegetables are tender. Remove rosemary sprig and discard.
2. Puree soup in small batches in a food processor or blender. To serve, return soup to pan and reheat. Ladle into bowls and sprinkle with freshly ground black pepper.
Fat per serve: 1 gram

Note: This soup is good served with toasted focaccia bread. Add 3 grams of fat for each average-sized piece.

> HINT
> Take care not to over-fill the food processor or blender when pureeing hot soup. Process in batches to prevent scalding hot liquid overflowing onto hands or bench.

Sweet Potato, Pumpkin and Orange Soup

Chicken Noodle Soup

Preparation time:
10 minutes
Total cooking time:
25 minutes
Serves 4

6 coriander stems, including leaves and roots
1.5 litres chicken stock
6 dried Kaffir lime leaves
1 teaspoon chopped fresh ginger
2 small (250 g) chicken breast fillets, skinned and thinly sliced
175 g fine dry Chinese egg noodles
1 teaspoon chopped fresh chilli
10 spring onions, cut into 2.5 cm lengths
200 g bean sprouts
1 tablespoon fish sauce

1. Cut roots from coriander; remove leaves, reserve 1/2 cup leaves. Place stock, coriander roots, lime leaves and ginger in a large pan; bring to the boil, cover and simmer for 10 minutes. Strain stock and reserve; discard solids.
2. Return stock to pan, add chicken and bring to boil. Reduce heat and simmer 3 minutes.
3. Break noodles into 3 cm pieces, add to pan with chilli and spring onion. Simmer until noodles are cooked—about 3 minutes. Add sprouts and fish sauce, stir gently until just heated through. Do not overcook—bean sprouts should be crisp.
4. Divide coriander leaves into bowls, ladle soup on top and serve.
Fat per serve: 3 grams

Potato, Leek and Spinach Soup

Preparation time:
20 minutes
Total cooking time:
35 minutes
Serves 4

2 teaspoons olive oil
1 medium onion, peeled and chopped
1 clove garlic, crushed
1 teaspoon dried thyme leaves
2 large leeks
400 g peeled potatoes, chopped roughly
4 cups chicken stock
1 bunch English spinach, washed and shredded
1/2 cup skim milk powder
juice of half a lemon

1. Heat oil in a large pan. Add onion, garlic and thyme, cover and cook over low heat for 3–4 minutes, stirring occasionally.
2. Cut leeks into thin slices, including the white and pale green portions but discarding the tough outer dark green leaves. Add leek and potato to the onion, cover and cook for another 3–4 minutes, stirring once or twice.
3. Add stock, bring to the boil and simmer for about 20 minutes, or until potatoes are almost tender.
4. Add the spinach and cook for another 3–4 minutes.
5. Process soup in batches in a food processor or blender, gradually adding skim milk powder during processing. Serve soup hot, or cool then refrigerate for several hours and serve cold. Just before serving, squeeze a little lemon juice into each bowl. Garnish with sliced lemon, if desired.
Fat per serve: 3 grams

Chicken Noodle Soup (top) and Potato, Leek and Spinach Soup

Vegetable Soup with Pesto

Preparation time:
15 minutes + overnight soaking
Total cooking time:
1 hour
Serves 6

1 cup dried white beans
2 teaspoons olive oil
2 medium onions, sliced finely
1 clove garlic, crushed
1 teaspoon dried thyme leaves
2 litres chicken stock
2 medium potatoes, peeled and cut into cubes
1 large leek, cleaned and sliced
1 medium carrot, sliced
2 cups peeled and cubed butternut pumpkin
2 cups sliced zucchini
2 cups sliced green beans
pepper, to taste

Pesto
large bunch fresh basil
2 cloves garlic, peeled
2 tablespoons lemon juice
1 tablespoon extra virgin olive oil
2 tablespoons pine nuts
2 tablespoons finely grated parmesan cheese

1. Place beans in large bowl; cover with cold water, soak overnight.
2. Drain beans and discard soaking water. Place beans in a large pan and add 1 1/2 litres cold water; bring to the boil, cover and leave to simmer for 40 minutes (do not overcook). Drain beans, discarding the water.
3. In a large pan, heat oil, add onion, garlic and thyme; cover and cook over low heat for 5 minutes (do not allow onions to colour). Add stock, white beans, potato, leek, carrot and pumpkin; bring to boil, cover and simmer for 7–8 minutes.
4. Add the zucchini and green beans and pepper, simmer another 3–4 minutes. Ladle soup into deep, heated serving bowls and top each bowl with a spoonful of Pesto.
To make Pesto: Strip basil leaves and place in a food processor with garlic, lemon juice and oil. Process until finely chopped. Add pine nuts and parmesan and process until smooth.
Fat per serve: 10 grams

Note: There is less oil in this pesto than in a true pesto, but enough to give it flavour.

Vegetable Soup with Pesto (top) and Green Pea Soup

Green Pea Soup

Preparation time:
15 minutes
Total cooking time:
15 minutes
Serves 4

1 litre chicken stock
500 g frozen peas
6 spring onions, sliced
3 or 4 large outside leaves of lettuce, washed well
1 teaspoon sugar
1 large or 2 small sprigs fresh rosemary
1/2 cup mint sprigs
juice of 1 lemon
1/2 cup low-fat natural yoghurt
black pepper

1. Heat stock in a large pan; add peas, spring onion, lettuce, sugar, rosemary and mint. Bring to boil, cover and simmer for 5 minutes (do not overcook or the fresh green colour will be lost). Remove rosemary and mint.
2. Place soup in food processor or blender and process until smooth. Return soup to pan and reheat.
3. Ladle soup into bowls. Squeeze a little lemon juice into each bowl. Swirl a spoonful of yoghurt into each serve and sprinkle with ground black pepper. Serve immediately.
Fat per serve: 1 gram

Seafood Soup

Preparation time:
15 minutes
Total cooking time:
45 minutes
Serves 4

500–750 g fish bones or 1 fish head
1 litre cold water
1 medium-sized carrot, chopped roughly
3 bay leaves
few sprigs parsley
1 teaspoon dried mixed herbs
1/2 lemon
2 teaspoons olive oil
1 large onion, sliced finely
2 cloves garlic, crushed
1 leek, cleaned and sliced
500 g potatoes, peeled and cut into cubes
350 g boneless fish fillets, cubed
500 g mussels in shell, scrubbed, beards removed
500 g green prawns, shelled and deveined
2 tablespoons lemon juice
1/2 cup freshly chopped coriander or parsley

1. In a large pan, place fish bones or head, water, carrot, bay leaves, parsley sprigs, mixed herbs and lemon. Bring to the boil, cover and simmer for 20 minutes. Strain fish stock, reserve liquid and discard solids.
2. Wash and dry pan. Heat oil and add the onion and garlic. Cook over low heat for 3–4 minutes. Add leek and potato and stir gently to combine. Cover and cook over low heat for 2–3 minutes. Add fish stock, bring to boil and simmer 12–15 minutes, or until potato is cooked.
3. Add fish fillets and bring back to boil. Add mussels, cook for a few minutes or until mussels open and fish is cooked (discard any unopened mussels).
4. Add prawns and cook until they just turn pink. Add lemon juice and coriander and serve at once. Garnish soup with a sprig of coriander, if desired.
Fat per serve: 5 grams

Note: This makes a wonderful dish for a weekend lunch or an evening meal. Serve with crusty French bread or warm Turkish pide bread.

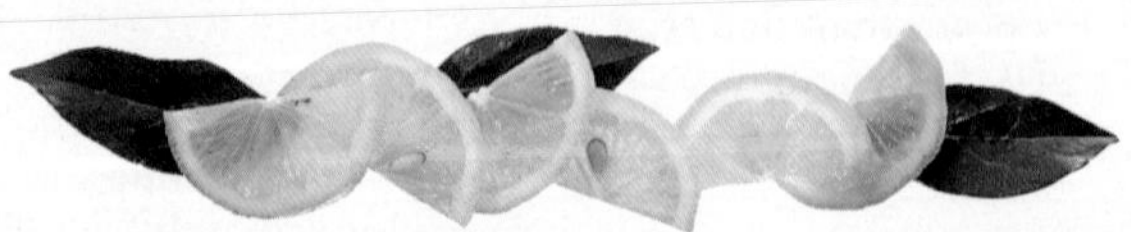

Seafood Soup

Breakfast Fruit Soup

Preparation time: 5 minutes + 30 minutes soaking
Total cooking time: 15 minutes
Serves 4–6

750 ml apple juice
1 cup dried peaches, cut into quarters
1 cup dried apples
1 cup prunes
1 cinnamon stick
1 vanilla bean
1/2 cup short-grain white rice
250 ml orange juice
250 ml peach juice
200 g low-fat natural yoghurt
1 teaspoon ground cinnamon
2 teaspoons sugar
2 oranges, peeled and sliced
sprigs of fresh mint, for serving

1. In a large pan, combine apple juice, dried peaches, apples and prunes, cinnamon stick, vanilla bean and rice. Set aside to soak for 30 minutes.
2. Bring the mixture to boil and simmer for 15 minutes. Cool and remove cinnamon stick and vanilla bean (do not worry about any black specks from the vanilla bean).
3. Add orange and peach juice and mix well. Add yoghurt, swirling lightly to give a striped effect (do not mix in completely).
4. Combine ground cinnamon and sugar in a cup. Serve soup chilled in bowls, topped with orange slices and sprinkled with cinnamon and sugar mixture. Garnish with mint sprigs.
Fat per serve: 0

Beetroot Soup

Preparation time: 15 minutes
Total cooking time: 15 minutes
Serves 4

2 teaspoons olive oil
1 medium onion, chopped
4 medium-sized fresh beetroot, peeled and grated
1 Granny Smith apple, peeled, cored and sliced
1 cup shredded red cabbage
4 cups chicken stock
2 tablespoons tomato puree
1/2 cup white wine
200 g low-fat natural yoghurt
finely chopped chives or parsley, to garnish

1. Heat oil in a large saucepan. Add onion and cook over low heat for 4–5 minutes, stirring occasionally.
2. Add the beetroot, apple, cabbage, stock and tomato puree; bring to the boil, cover and simmer for 10 minutes. Add the wine. If serving soup hot, serve at once. If serving cold, allow to cool and then refrigerate for at least 2 hours. To serve, ladle the soup into four serving bowls and top each with a dollop of yoghurt. Swirl through with a fork if desired and garnish with chives or parsley.
Fat per serve: 3 grams

> HINT
> The flavour of fresh beetroot is very refreshing and lifts this soup out of the ordinary. If you can't find fresh beetroot, use an 810 g can of sliced beetroot (drained). Serve soup hot in winter, chilled in summer.

Beetroot Soup (top) and Breakfast Fruit Soup

Salads & Vegetables

You can be very creative with vegetables, whether using them in salads or hot dishes. The recipes in this section are easy to make and delicious and each contains just a little fat—between 1 and 6 grams only.

Mediterranean Salad

Preparation time:
15 minutes + 20 minutes standing + 30 minutes refrigeration
Total cooking time:
15 minutes
Serves 4

1 medium eggplant, about 500 g, cut into 6 mm (1/4 inch) slices
salt
1 tablespoon olive oil
1 large red onion, sliced finely
1 clove garlic, crushed
1 teaspoon dried oregano leaves
1 red capsicum, seeded and sliced
1 green capsicum, seeded and sliced
3–4 medium tomatoes
1 tablespoon capers
2 tablespoons balsamic vinegar
ground black pepper

1. Sprinkle eggplant slices with salt. Set aside for 20 minutes.
2. Heat the oil in a non-stick pan; add onion, garlic, oregano and capsicum, cover and cook over low heat—do not brown.
3. Place tomatoes in heatproof bowl, pour boiling water over and leave for 2 minutes. Drain tomatoes and plunge them into cold water. Peel skins from tops downwards. Slice tomatoes and place in a large bowl. Add onion and capsicum mixture, and capers.
4. Rinse eggplant, pat dry with paper towel. Place under hot grill until slices are just turning brown; grill other side. Cut into pieces, add to tomato mixture. Sprinkle vinegar over vegetables; add pepper, toss well and refrigerate 30 minutes to allow

Mediterranean Salad

flavours to blend. Sprinkle with chopped parsley and serve with crusty bread, or as a topping for toast.
Fat per serve: 5 grams

Note: Sliced zucchini or sliced mushrooms can be added to this recipe, if desired.

Herbed Pasta Salad

Preparation time: 15 minutes + refrigeration
Total cooking time: 10 minutes
Serves 4

375 g pasta spirals
1 tablespoon olive oil
2 cloves garlic, crushed
6 spring onions, finely sliced (1 cup)
4 anchovy fillets, chopped roughly
1 large carrot, cut into fine strips
8 black olives, thinly sliced
1–2 tablespoons lemon juice
1 cup chopped fresh basil
1/4 cup chopped fresh coriander
2 tablespoons chopped fresh mint

1. Bring a large pan of water to boil, add pasta and cook until just tender. Drain well.
2. While the pasta is cooking, heat the oil in a medium pan and cook garlic and spring onion for 1 minute; remove from heat. Add anchovies, carrot, olives, lemon juice and herbs; mix well.
3. Add mixture to hot, drained pasta and toss well; cool. Refrigerate until cold and serve.
Fat per serve: 6 grams

Lemon and Honey Stir-fry

Preparation time: 10 minutes
Total cooking time: 15 minutes
Serves 4

2 teaspoons sesame oil
1 medium onion, cut into eighths
1 clove garlic, crushed
1 teaspoon chopped chilli
1 teaspoon chopped fresh ginger
1 tablespoon honey
8 cups sliced vegetables (broccoli, cauliflower, zucchini, pumpkin, green beans, fresh asparagus, snow peas, mushrooms, capsicum)
1/2 cup chicken stock
1 tablespoon soy sauce
1 tablespoon lemon juice

1. Heat oil in wok or large non-stick frying pan and cook onion for 3–4 minutes.
2. Add garlic, chilli, ginger and honey and toss well to combine.
3. Add vegetables and stir-fry until vegetables are just tender—about 10–12 minutes.
4. Combine stock, soy sauce and lemon juice and pour over vegetables. Increase heat to High and toss ingredients together until vegetables are well coated. Serve with steamed rice.
Fat per serve: 3 grams

> HINT
> You can vary the vegetables used for this dish. It's a good way to use up small leftover quantities —but only if they are still fresh. Wilted produce will give a poor result.

Lemon and Honey Stir-fry (top) and Herbed Pasta Salad

Roasted Vegetables

Preparation time: 15 minutes
Total cooking time: 25 minutes
Serves 4

2 red capsicums
4 small onions
4 medium-sized tomatoes
4 sprigs fresh rosemary
2 small bulbs fennel
2 bulbs garlic
2 teaspoons olive oil
freshly ground black pepper

1. Preheat oven to moderately hot 200°C. Halve capsicums lengthways and remove seeds and membrane; peel onions. Cut tomatoes in halves without cutting through the stem end; insert a sprig of rosemary into each and close tomato around it.

2. Cut fennel bulbs in half lengthways; cut garlic bulbs in half crossways so cut end of each clove is visible. Brush fennel and garlic with olive oil.

3. Place vegetables in a roasting pan and bake for 25 minutes. Remove from oven, squeeze roasted garlic over fennel. Sprinkle with ground black pepper, garnish with flat-leaf parsley, if desired Serve at once with grilled fish, chicken or lean meat, or slices of grilled ricotta.

Fat per serve: 3 grams

Roasted Vegetables

1 Cut capsicums in half lengthways and remove seeds and membrane.

2 Cut garlic bulbs in half crossways to expose cloves.

3 *Arrange the vegetables in a roasting pan and bake for 25 minutes.*

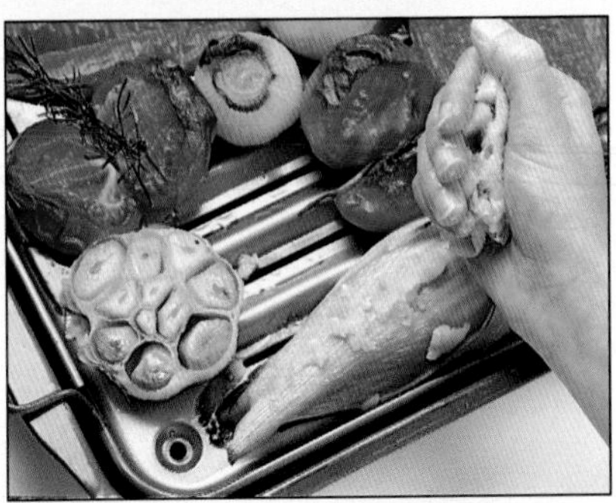

4 *Remove vegetables from the oven and squeeze roasted garlic over the fennel.*

Warm Pumpkin Salad

Preparation time:
15 minutes
Total cooking time:
20 minutes
Serves 4

1 tablespoon sesame seeds
2 teaspoons olive oil
1 small onion, finely sliced
1 medium fennel bulb, sliced finely
500 g peeled pumpkin, preferably butternut, cut into 6 mm (1/4 inch) slices
1/4 cup orange juice
2 teaspoons lemon juice
2 teaspoons honey
1 teaspoon sesame oil
2 teaspoons finely grated orange rind
2 tablespoons chopped fresh chives

1. Toast sesame seeds in a frying pan until golden (take care not to burn). Remove from heat and set aside.
2. Heat olive oil in pan, add onion and fennel, cover and cook over low heat 3–4 minutes.
3. Add pumpkin and continue cooking, turning gently until just tender. Transfer to a shallow dish.
4. Combine orange and lemon juices, honey, sesame oil and orange rind. Pour over pumpkin and sprinkle with chives.
Fat per serve: 5 grams

Note: Pumpkin makes an unusual but tasty salad ingredient. Do not overcook—slices should be firm.

Minted Cracked Wheat Salad

Preparation time:
15 minutes + 30 minutes standing
Total cooking time:
Nil
Serves 4

1 cup cracked wheat (burghul)
1/2 cup chopped dried apricots
2 cups boiling water
1 telegraph cucumber, or 2–3 Lebanese cucumbers
1 cup chopped mint
1/2 cup chopped parsley
1/2 cup chopped fresh coriander
1 small red onion, very finely chopped
1/2 cup finely chopped spring onions
2 tablespoons lemon juice
8 lettuce cups

1. Place cracked wheat and dried apricots in a bowl or pan with a tight-fitting lid. Pour boiling water over, cover and leave to stand for 15 minutes (the water will be absorbed).
2. Peel cucumbers and cut in half lengthways. Using a teaspoon, scoop out seeds and discard. Slice cucumbers finely and set aside to drain well for 15 minutes. Pat dry with paper towel, if necessary.
3. Add cucumber, mint, parsley, coriander, onion, spring onion and lemon juice to cracked wheat mixture; mix together and fluff with a fork.
4. Serve salad in lettuce cups, accompanied by flat Lebanese bread and some sliced ripe tomatoes. Garnish with parsley if desired.
Fat per serve: 1 gram

Warm Pumpkin Salad (top) and Minted Cracked Wheat Salad

Black-eyed Beans with Leeks

Preparation time:
5 minutes
Total cooking time:
1 hour
Serves 4

250 g black-eyed beans
4 cups water
2 leeks, washed well
2 teaspoons olive oil
1 clove garlic, crushed
1 tablespoon grainy mustard
1 cup cider
1 tablespoon fresh lemon thyme, or 1 teaspoon dried thyme leaves
2 tablespoons chopped fresh parsley

1. Place beans in a large pan and cover with water. Bring to boil, reduce heat and simmer for about 40 minutes.
2. Slice leeks (white and tender green parts only; discard tough, outer green leaves).
3. Heat oil in a large pan, add garlic and leek and cook, covered, over low heat 4–5 minutes, stirring occasionally.
4. Add the mustard, cider, drained beans and thyme to the garlic and leek mixture; cover and continue cooking for about 15 minutes, or until beans are tender but not mushy. Sprinkle with parsley and serve.
Fat per serve: 4 grams

> **Hint**
> Black-eyed beans are small and don't need soaking. If beans give you wind, soak them overnight. Pour off water, replace with fresh water. Cook for 25 minutes.

Black-eyed Beans with Leeks

1 Place the black-eyed beans in a large pan with enough water to cover.

2 Cut the leeks into slices, discarding the tough outer leaves.

3 Heat the oil in a large pan and cook garlic and leek.

4 Add the mustard, cider, drained beans and thyme to the pan.

Potato Salad with Basil Yoghurt Dressing

Preparation time: 10 minutes + refrigeration
Total cooking time: 5–10 minutes
Serves 4

500 g new (cocktail) potatoes
2 tablespoons lemon juice
200 g natural low-fat yoghurt
1 clove garlic, crushed
1 cup chopped fresh basil
1/2 cup chopped fresh parsley
freshly ground black pepper
1 tablespoon toasted pine nuts

1. Scrub potatoes if necessary and steam or microwave until tender. While potatoes are still hot, cut each into halves (if small) or quarters and sprinkle with lemon juice.
2. Combine yoghurt, garlic, basil, parsley and plenty of black pepper. Add to warm potatoes and toss gently. Cool, refrigerate. Just before serving, sprinkle with toasted pine nuts. Serve with wholemeal bread and a salad made from different types of lettuce, watercress and baby spinach leaves. Add some cherry tomatoes or baby beetroot, if desired.
Fat per serve: 3 grams

Ratatouille

Preparation time: 25 minutes + 20 minutes standing
Total cooking time: 40 minutes
Serves 4

1 medium eggplant, chopped
4 large tomatoes
1 tablespoon olive oil
2 medium onions, chopped
2 cloves garlic, crushed
1 green capsicum, seeded and chopped
1 red capsicum, seeded and chopped
4 large zucchini, sliced
1 teaspoon dried oregano leaves
2 large bay leaves

1. Sprinkle eggplant with salt and set aside for 20 minutes. Rinse and pat dry with paper towel. Score a cross in base of each tomato, place in large heatproof bowl and cover with boiling water. Leave to stand for 3–4 minutes, then remove from bowl and cool. Peel skins away and roughly chop tomato flesh.
2. Heat oil in a large pan, cook onion over low heat for 15 minutes until very soft, stirring occasionally. Add garlic, cook another minute.
3. Add eggplant, capsicum and zucchini. Increase heat to medium and cook for another 5 minutes, stirring occasionally. Add tomato, oregano and bay leaves, reduce heat, cover and simmer for 15 minutes. Uncover and cook for another 5 minutes until thickened slightly. Serve either hot or at room temperature.
Fat per serve: 5 grams

> **Hint**
> This is delicious stuffed into pitta bread, or with grilled fish or chicken. For a delicious, low-fat variation, make a few hollows in the ratatouille in the pan and break an egg into each. Cook until eggs are set.

Ratatouille (top) and Potato Salad with Basil Yoghurt Dressing

Basil-stuffed Tomatoes

Preparation time:
20 minutes
Total cooking time:
20 minutes
Serves 6

6 medium-sized ripe tomatoes
1 large bunch basil (about 2 cups leaves)
2 tablespoons chopped fresh chives
2 cloves garlic, crushed
2 tablespoons lemon juice
250 g ricotta cheese
salt and pepper, to taste
2 slices wholemeal bread, made into breadcrumbs
2 tablespoons grated parmesan cheese
1 tablespoon chopped parsley

1. Preheat the oven to moderate 180°C. Cut a lid from the top of each tomato, scoop out the flesh and turn tomatoes upside-down to drain. Chop the tomato flesh and drain in a small colander. (Save the tomato juices and use later to flavour stocks.)
2. Place the basil leaves, chives, garlic and lemon juice in a blender or food processor and process until all ingredients are well combined. Add the ricotta, salt and pepper, and chopped tomato flesh; mix well.
3. Spoon the filling mixture into the tomato shells and top with breadcrumbs. Place in a shallow casserole dish and bake for 15–20 minutes. Sprinkle with parsley and serve.
Fat per serve: 5 grams

Note: Make sure you leave a thick enough wall so the tomato does not burst when filled.

> Hint
> Serve Basil-stuffed Tomatoes with some good Italian bread or crusty wholemeal rolls to make a simple meal. Or serve with grilled lamb or fish.

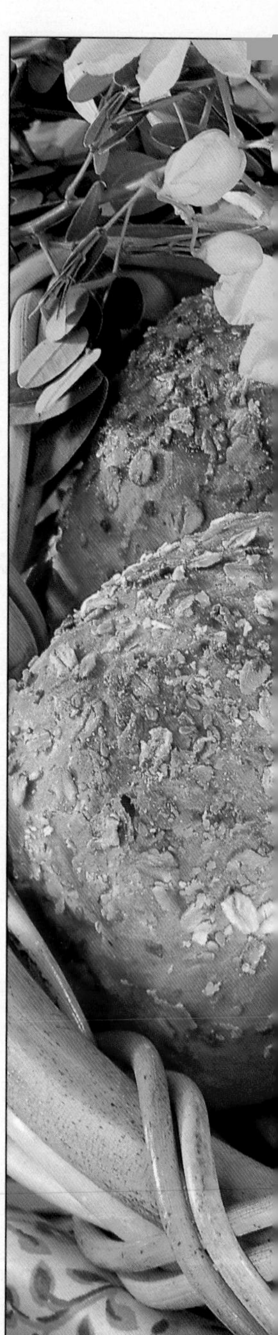

Basil-stuffed Tomatoes

Something Light

Grain-based meals are filling, delicious and inexpensive—even the finest pasta, or a special rice such as arborio, usually costs less than the cheapest meat you can buy. These dishes contain between 1 and 7 grams of fat per serve. Add lots of vegetables, salads and fresh bread to make a complete meal.

Fettuccine and Greens

Preparation time: 20 minutes
Total cooking time: 15–20 minutes
Serves 4

1 tablespoon olive oil
2 cloves garlic, finely chopped
4 anchovy fillets, thoroughly drained and chopped
1 fresh chilli, seeded and sliced
500 g broccoli
1 bunch fresh asparagus, cut into 3 cm lengths
1 bunch arugula (rocket), sliced
500 g fettuccine
freshly ground black pepper
sliced fresh chilli, to serve

1. Place the oil, garlic, anchovy and chilli in a large frying pan and cook over very low heat for 1–2 minutes.

2. Discard coarse broccoli stems and slice remaining stems thinly. Divide broccoli into small florets. Add florets with stem slices to the pan and stir-fry for 2–3 minutes.

3. Add asparagus and rocket to the pan and continue stir-frying for a couple of minutes more, until asparagus is just cooked through.

4. While vegetables are cooking, bring a large pan of water to boil and cook fettuccine until just tender; do not overcook. Drain pasta quickly (leave a little water behind to help keep the pasta moist). Turn drained fettuccine into a deep, heated bowl and top with

Fettuccine and Greens

plenty of ground black pepper, toss well and serve immediately, garnished with fine strips of fresh chilli.
Fat per serve: 7 grams

Note: Watercress or English spinach may be used instead of rocket in this recipe, if you dislike the taste of rocket. Wear disposable gloves when preparing chilli and do not rub your eyes afterwards. To serve four, 375 g of pasta is usually enough, but allow 500 g for larger appetites.

Fusili with Tuna

Preparation time:
20 minutes
Total cooking time:
15 minutes
Serves 6

400 g fusili (spiral or twist noodles)
1 tablespoon olive oil
10 spring onions, chopped
500 g button mushrooms, quartered
2 cloves garlic, crushed
425 g can tuna in spring water, drained and flaked
2 teaspoons finely grated lemon rind
2 tablespoons lemon juice
1/3 cup chopped parsley
1/3 cup chopped chives

1. Bring a large pan of water to the boil and cook fusili until tender.
2. While the pasta is cooking, heat oil in a medium pan and add the spring onion and mushrooms. Stir over medium heat for 3–4 minutes, until the onion and mushrooms have softened.
3. Add the garlic to the pan and cook for one minute longer.
4. Drain the pasta, return it to the pan and add the onion and mushroom mixture, tuna, lemon rind and juice, and parsley and chives. Toss until well combined and warmed through. Serve immediately. Garnish with celery curls, if desired.
Fat per serve: 6 grams

Hint
If you prefer, canned pink or red salmon can be substituted for the tuna in this recipe.

Tofu with Noodles

Preparation time:
10 minutes
Total cooking time:
15 minutes
Serves 4

4 or 5 dried Chinese mushrooms
1 cup water
4 cups chicken stock
1 cup broccoli pieces
2 cups sliced Chinese greens
250 g fine rice noodles, soaked in warm water for 5 minutes and drained
1 cup sliced green spring onions
2 cups bean sprouts
200 g bean curd (tofu), cut into 1 cm cubes
1 tablespoon light soy sauce
1 teaspoon sesame oil

1. Soak dried mushrooms in water for 20 minutes. Cut into strips. Discard the water.
2. Bring stock to boil, add mushrooms and broccoli. Simmer for 5 minutes.
3. Add greens and noodles, simmer for another 3–4 minutes. Add spring onion, bean sprouts and bean curd; simmer for 2 minutes.
4. Sprinkle with soy sauce and sesame oil and serve immediately.
Fat per serve: 4 grams.

Fusili with Tuna (top) and Tofu with Noodles

Grilled Polenta with Roasted Capsicum

Preparation time:
25 minutes
Total cooking time:
35 minutes
Serves 4

1 red capsicum
1 green capsicum
1 yellow capsicum
4 cups chicken stock
pinch salt
1 cup polenta (cornmeal)
1 tablespoon balsamic vinegar
4 egg tomatoes

1. Cut capsicums in half and place, cut-side down, on grill plate. Grill under hot grill until the skin blisters and blackens. Remove from grill and cover with a damp tea towel for 2–3 minutes.
2. While capsicums are roasting, place stock and salt in a large heavy-based pan. Bring to the boil then add the polenta in a slow, steady stream, stirring constantly (use a wooden spoon as plastic ones may break when the mixture thickens). Cook over medium heat, stirring, for 20 minutes. Pour hot polenta into a 20 cm square cake tin that has been rinsed in cold water. Leave until set (about 15 minutes).
3. While polenta is setting, peel skin from capsicums and discard. Cut flesh into strips, place in a bowl and sprinkle with balsamic vinegar and any juices from capsicum.
4. Cut tomatoes into thin slices. Turn polenta out of tin, cut into slices and grill slices under a hot grill until brown. Serve topped with roasted capsicum strips and tomato. Sprinkle with cracked black pepper.
Fat per serve: 2 grams

HINT
Polenta has very little fat. It takes a little time to cook, but the result is worth it. It is one of the few dishes in which I use salt, but its flavour seems to need the lift of a little salt.

Grilled Polenta with Roasted Capsicum

Simple Spaghetti

Preparation time:
10 minutes
Total cooking time:
20 minutes
Serves 4

2 teaspoons olive oil
1 onion, finely chopped
2–3 cloves garlic, crushed
1/2 cup chopped parsley
2 teaspoons dried oregano, or 1 tablespoon fresh oregano, chopped
800 g canned tomatoes
2 tablespoons tomato paste
1/2 cup good red wine
500 g spaghetti
2 tablespoons capers
12 black olives
1/2 cup chopped parsley, extra
2 tablespoons chopped fresh basil

1. Heat oil and cook onion, garlic, parsley and oregano for 1–2 minutes over low heat.
2. Add tomatoes with their juice, tomato paste and wine and bring to the boil. Cover and simmer 5 minutes, stirring to break up tomatoes.
3. Cook the spaghetti in a large pan of boiling water until just tender; do not overcook.
4. Add capers and olives to tomato sauce and serve over drained spaghetti. Sprinkle with extra parsley and basil.
Fat per serve: 5 grams

Risotto with Zucchini and Capsicum

Preparation time:
10 minutes
Total cooking time:
35 minutes
Serves 4

2 teaspoons olive oil
2–3 cloves garlic, finely chopped
1 onion, finely chopped
500 g zucchini, sliced
1 red capsicum, seeded and sliced
2 or 3 sprigs fresh rosemary, or 1 teaspoon dried
350 g (2 cups) Arborio rice
1/2 cup white wine
5 1/2 cups hot chicken stock
2 tablespoons finely grated parmesan cheese
2 tablespoons chopped fresh oregano
2 tablespoons chopped fresh parsley

1. Place oil, garlic and onion in a heavy-based pan, cover and cook over low heat for 2–3 minutes.
2. Add zucchini, capsicum, rosemary and rice and stir for 2–3 minutes.
3. Add wine and 1/2 cup of stock, bring to boil. Simmer until most of the liquid has been absorbed. Continue adding stock, one cup at a time, until all is absorbed and rice is just tender (about 20–25 minutes).
4. Add parmesan and herbs and stir gently with a fork. Serve immediately, sprinkled with cracked black pepper. Garnish with oregano, if desired.
Fat per serve: 5 grams

HINT
Any short-grained rice can be used to make risotto but it may not give the authentic creamy result. Arborio, an Italian short-grained rice that absorbs a lot of water without going soggy, is best.

Simple Spaghetti (top) and Risotto with Zucchini and Capsicum

Couscous with Vegetables

Preparation time: 20 minutes
Total cooking time: 20 minutes
Serves 4

1 cup couscous
2 cups boiling water
2 teaspoons olive oil
1 medium onion, cut into eighths
1 teaspoon chopped fresh ginger
pinch saffron
1 cinnamon stick
1 1/2 cups chicken stock
1 large carrot, cut into chunks
250 g frozen peas
250 g butternut pumpkin, peeled and sliced
400 g can chickpeas, or 1 cup cooked chickpeas, drained
2–3 medium zucchini, cut into chunks
1/4 cup fresh parsley

1. Place couscous into a medium pan, pour boiling water over, cover tightly and leave to stand for about 10–15 minutes (do not lift the lid).
2. Heat oil and cook onion, ginger and saffron over low heat for 2–3 minutes. Add cinnamon stick, chicken stock and carrot. Bring to the boil, cover and simmer for 5 minutes.
3. Add peas, pumpkin, chickpeas and zucchini and continue cooking until the pumpkin is just tender. Stir in the parsley. Remove the cinnamon stick and discard it.
4. Fluff up the couscous with a fork and place on a serving plate. Arrange vegetables on top. Pour any of the remaining liquid over the vegetables and serve immediately.
Fat per serve: 4 grams

HINT
Couscous is a staple of North African cuisine, found in most supermarkets. To prepare it by a more authentic method, place in a fine strainer and run cold water through to wet grains. Place in a large shallow bowl and sprinkle with 1 cup water. Leave 10 minutes, then roll grains with fingertips, breaking up all lumps and allowing water to be absorbed. Place in steamer over boiling water or stock, cover tightly, steam about 20 minutes.

Couscous with Vegetables

1 Pour boiling water over the couscous in a medium pan.

2 Add cinnamon stick, stock and carrots to onion, ginger and saffron.

3 Cook until the pumpkin is just tender, then stir in the parsley.

4 Remove lid from pan and fluff up the soaked couscous with a fork.

Rice Pie

Preparation time: 25 minutes
Total cooking time: 1 hour 15 minutes
Serves 4

3/4 cup brown rice
1 1/2 cups water
150 g grated low-fat cheddar (7% fat)
1/2 cup chopped fresh mint
1/2 cup spring onions, sliced
1 red capsicum, seeded and finely chopped
1 large carrot, grated
2 or 3 zucchini, grated
1 cup drained canned corn kernels
3 eggs, beaten
1/2 cup low-fat yoghurt
1 teaspoon paprika

1. Preheat oven to 180°C. Brush a 23 cm pie dish lightly with oil. Combine rice and water in a large pan; bring to boil, cover, lower heat and simmer 25 minutes, or until all water is absorbed. Transfer rice to a bowl, cool for 5 minutes.
2. Add remaining ingredients, except paprika, to rice. Press into prepared dish; sprinkle with paprika. Bake for 50 minutes. Remove from oven and leave for 5 minutes before serving, or cool and refrigerate if serving cold. Serve hot with steamed vegetables or cold with a salad. Garnish with fresh herbs, if desired.
Fat per serve: 5 grams

Salad Loaf

Preparation time: 10 minutes + 30 minutes refrigeration
Total cooking time: 25 minutes
Serves 4

2 red capsicums
1 French bread stick
1 tablespoon grain mustard
185 g can tuna in water or brine, drained
2 tablespoons capers
1/2 cup chopped parsley
1 tablespoon lemon juice
1/2 cup low-fat yoghurt
8 lettuce leaves (oak leaf, butter or coral lettuce)
4 cold boiled potatoes, sliced
2 hard-boiled eggs, sliced
freshly ground black pepper

1. Preheat oven to hot 250°C. Place whole capsicums on oven shelf and cook for 25 minutes (the skin will blister and may blacken). Remove from oven, leave to cool for a few minutes, then peel off skin. Cut in halves, remove seeds and slice roasted capsicum flesh into strips.
2. Cut french stick in half horizontally (for a picnic, toast on a barbecue before filling if you like) and spread bottom half lightly with mustard.
3. Combine tuna, capers, parsley, lemon juice and yoghurt. Place lettuce leaves over mustard on bread stick. Top with tuna mixture, potato, eggs and capsicum and sprinkle with plenty of black pepper.
4. Place remaining bread on top. Wrap firmly in plastic wrap and refrigerate for at least 30 minutes. To serve, cut into 4 portions.
Fat per serve: 6 grams

> **Hint**
> Add some thinly sliced red onion to Salad Loaf if you like onions. Salmon can be substituted for tuna if you prefer—fat content will increase to 8 grams per serve.

Salad Loaf (top) and Rice Pie

Pilau with Onions and Almonds

Preparation time:
10 minutes
Total cooking time:
45 minutes–1 hour
Serves 2–4

1 tablespoon olive oil
2 medium onions, thinly sliced
1 cup rice, brown or white
2 tablespoons raisins
2 cups water
1 tablespoon slivered almonds
1/2 cup chopped fresh coriander
2 tablespoons chopped fresh chives or oregano
salt and pepper, to taste

1. Heat oil in a large heavy-based pan and cook onion, covered, over low heat, stirring occasionally, for 20 minutes.
2. Add rice and raisins, stir for 2–3 minutes. Add water and bring to boil; cover, turn heat to low and cook for 20 minutes (for white rice) or 30–40 minutes (for brown rice).
3. While rice is cooking, toast almonds: spread in a dry frying pan and place over low heat until nuts have turned golden brown. Set aside.
4. When rice is cooked, add the almonds, coriander, and chives or oregano; toss lightly to combine. Season to serve, garnish with oregano, if desired.
Fat per serve: 7 grams

Herbed Bread

Preparation time:
35 minutes + 1 1/2 hours standing
Total cooking time:
25 minutes
Serves 6

7 g sachet dried yeast
1 teaspoon sugar
1 1/4 cups lukewarm water
4–5 sundried tomatoes
3 cups plain flour
pinch salt
1 red capsicum, seeded and finely chopped
2 teaspoons dried rosemary leaves
2 teaspoons dried oregano leaves
2 tablespoons fresh chopped chives
2 teaspoons olive oil

1. Brush an oven tray lightly with oil. Combine yeast and sugar and add a little of the water. Mix well. Add remaining water. Leave in warm place for about 5 minutes until frothy. Soak tomatoes in boiling water 5–10 minutes or until soft. Drain, chop finely.
2. Sift flour and salt into a large bowl, make a well in centre. Add yeast mixture, mix to form a soft dough. Add more flour if needed.
3. Turn dough onto a lightly floured surface and knead for about 10 minutes or until it feels springy. Place into an oiled bowl, cover and leave in a warm place for about an hour, or until doubled in size.
4. Punch dough down and knead 2–3 minutes. Push dough out flat and sprinkle with capsicum, dried tomato and herbs. Roll up and then continue kneading until flavourings are well incorporated. Pat dough into a circle about 23 cm in diameter, place on prepared tray, brush with olive oil and score top of dough, if desired. Leave to rise for another 30 minutes.
5. Preheat oven to 200°C and bake bread for about 25 minutes. Cut into wedges and serve warm.
Fat per serve: 3 grams

Herbed Bread (top) and Pilau with Onions and Almonds

Main Courses

At the end of the day, vegetables, rice, pasta or other grains served with a small portion of lean meat, chicken or seafood, will meet the body's needs. The following recipes contain between 2 and 10 grams of fat per serve.

Grilled Chicken with Thai Herbs

Preparation time: 20 minutes
Total cooking time: 10 minutes
Serves 4

500 g chicken breast fillets
1 cup chopped mint (use Vietnamese mint, if available)
1/2 bunch coriander, chopped
1 cup chopped basil
1/2 green pawpaw, thinly sliced
8 kaffir lime leaves, finely shredded
1 teaspoon finely sliced lemon grass
2 teaspoons finely chopped ginger
1 or 2 chillies, seeded and finely sliced
1 tablespoon roasted peanuts, chopped
1 cup bean sprouts

Sauce
1/4 cup fresh lime juice
1 tablespoon palm sugar
1 1/2 tablespoons fish sauce

1. Place chicken fillets under preheated grill for about 10 minutes, or until just cooked.
2. Combine mint, coriander and basil, pawpaw, lime leaves, lemon grass, ginger, chillies, peanuts and bean sprouts in a medium bowl; mix well.
3. Place a mound of herb mixture on serving plate, top with chicken and sprinkle with sauce. Garnish with strips of red capsicum, if desired. Serve chicken immediately with steamed rice, stir-fried snow peas or green beans (use 1 teaspoon sesame oil to stir-fry enough for four serves). Garnish with capsicum strips, if desired.

Grilled Chicken with Thai Herbs

4. *To make Sauce:* Combine all ingredients in a small bowl.
Fat per serve for chicken dish: 6 grams. If adding stir-fried snow peas and rice, total fat content is 7 grams.

Seafood Hotpot

Preparation time: 20 minutes
Total cooking time: 15 minutes
Serves 4

400 g boneless white fish fillets
300 g green medium or king prawns
12 mussels
2 teaspoons olive oil
1 large onion, sliced
3 small zucchini, sliced
1 clove garlic, crushed
1 teaspoon dried thyme leaves
1 teaspoon dried rosemary leaves
800 g can tomatoes, chopped
1/2 cup white wine
1/2 cup chopped parsley
1/2 cup chopped fresh basil
2 tablespoons lemon juice

1. Cut fish into 2 cm chunks. Shell and devein the prawns, leaving tails intact. Scrub mussels and remove beards.
2. Heat oil in a large pan, add onion and zucchini and cook, stirring, over low heat for 5 minutes, until softened.
3. Add the garlic, thyme, rosemary, tomato and wine; bring to the boil and simmer, uncovered, 5 minutes. Add the fish and cook for 2 minutes, until flesh turns white.
4. Add prawns and mussels, cover and cook for another 3 minutes, until prawns are pink and mussels have opened. Stir in parsley, basil and juice. Garnish with parsley, if desired. Serve immediately, with crusty bread.
Fat per serve: 5 grams

Hint
Seafood Hotpot is delicious served with plain steamed potatoes. The added carbohydrate will make a substantial and satisfying meal.

Kingfish Steaks with Chermoula

Preparation time: 10 minutes
Total cooking time: 10 minutes
Serves 4

4 kingfish steaks

Chermoula
small bunch fresh coriander
1 cup parsley sprigs
2 cloves garlic
1/2 cup lemon juice
2 teaspoons grated lemon rind
1 teaspoon ground cumin
1 teaspoon ground paprika
ground black pepper

1. Cook kingfish under grill, on a barbecue or in a lightly greased non-stick pan until flesh just flakes (do not overcook). Serve with chermoula.
2. *To make Chermoula:* While fish is cooking, place all ingredients in food processor, process until well combined. Serve with fish.
Fat per serve: 2 grams

Note: Chermoula is a Moroccan sauce which can also be used as a marinade for fish.

Seafood Hotpot (top) and Kingfish Steaks with Chermoula

Stir-fried Pork and Noodles

Preparation time:
20 minutes
Total cooking time:
5–10 minutes
Serves 4

250 g fine rice noodles
2 cloves garlic
2 red chillies
1 tablespoon peanut or macadamia nut oil
1 medium onion, sliced
300 g lean pork steak or pork fillet, cut into strips
6–8 cups sliced vegetables (capsicum, broccoli, celery, cabbage, beans, asparagus, mushrooms, cauliflower, carrot, zucchini, Brussels sprouts, eggplant or spinach)
1 tablespoon light soy sauce
250 g bean sprouts

1. Place noodles in a large bowl and cover with boiling water. Leave for 5 minutes.
2. Pound the garlic and chillies together in a small mortar and pestle. (Remove chilli seeds if you don't like hot foods, but wear disposable gloves and don't touch your eyes).
3. Heat oil in wok or large pan; stir-fry chilli, onion and pork, tossing until pork is brown (about 5 minutes).
4. Add vegetables and stir-fry for 3–4 minutes.
5. Add soy sauce, bean sprouts and drained noodles; toss together until heated through.
Fat per serve: 7 grams

Tipsy Chicken with Vegetables

Preparation time:
20 minutes + 1 hour refrigeration
Total cooking time:
50–55 minutes
Serves 4

1/4 cup lime juice
2 teaspoons finely grated lime rind
2 tablespoons brandy
4 half chicken breasts, without skin (600 g)
1 small eggplant
2 red capsicums
1 green capsicum
1 clove garlic, crushed
3–4 teaspoons lemon juice
4 medium zucchini
4 large mushrooms, stems removed

Tipsy Chicken with Vegetables (top) and Stir-fried Pork and Noodles

1. Combine lime juice, lime rind and brandy. Pour over chicken, cover and refrigerate for at least an hour, preferably longer. Turn chicken once.
2. Preheat oven to hot 250°C. Prick eggplant with a skewer in several places and place capsicums and eggplant on oven shelf. Roast for 25–40 minutes. When cool enough to handle, remove blackened skin from capsicums, cut in half and remove core and seeds, reserving juices. (Vegetables can be prepared ahead to this stage, if desired.)
3. Cut eggplant in half and remove flesh. Mash with garlic and lemon juice and set aside.
4. Grill chicken for 10–15 minutes, turning once and brushing with marinade. Slice zucchini in halves lengthwise place zucchini and mushrooms under grill when chicken is turned.
5. While chicken is cooking, slice capsicums. To serve, place chicken on serving plates, top with 1/4 of mashed eggplant mixture, then a few strips of red and green capsicum. Serve zucchini and mushrooms on the side.
Fat per serve: 3 grams

Note: Overnight marinating makes this dish taste even better.

Lamb with Red Capsicum Sauce

Preparation time:
20 minutes
Total cooking time:
40 minutes
Serves 4

2 red capsicums
3 medium tomatoes, cored
1/4 teaspoon ground cumin
1 teaspoon ground coriander
1 teaspoon chopped chilli
freshly ground pepper
2 teaspoons chopped fresh mint
1 clove garlic
4 x 110 g lamb steaks, trimmed of fat
fresh coriander leaves, for serving

1. Preheat oven to hot 250°C. Place capsicums on oven shelf,bake for 15 minutes. Add tomatoes and cook another 10 minutes.
2. When cool enough to handle, remove blackened skin from capsicums and tomatoes. Place flesh in blender, or processor add cumin, coriander, chilli, pepper mint and garlic. Process until smooth; set aside.
3. Grill lamb steaks as desired. Place some roasted capsicum sauce on each plate, top with a grilled lamb steak. Add a few sprigs of fresh coriander. Serve with vegetables or salad.
Fat per serve: 7 grams. (If using dressing on salad, remember to add 12 grams of fat per tablespoon of dressing, or use a no-oil product and avoid adding fat.)

Osso Bucco

Preparation time:
20 minutes
Total cooking time:
2 1/2 hours
Serves 4

2 teaspoons olive oil
2 large veal shanks, cut into osso bucco
2 medium onions, chopped
1 leek, washed, sliced
2 cloves garlic, crushed
800 g can tomatoes, chopped
1 large eggplant, chopped
1 cup water
1 cup good red wine
2 bay leaves
1 teaspoon dried oregano leaves
1 teaspoon dried rosemary leaves
2 teaspoons finely grated lemon rind
1/2 cup chopped parsley
1 clove garlic, crushed, extra

1. Heat oil in a large heavy-based pan. Cook meat in two batches until well browned; transfer to a plate and set aside. Add onion and leek to pan and cook over medium heat for 10 minutes, stirring occasionally.
2. Add garlic to pan, cook for another minute. Return meat to pan, add tomato with liquid, eggplant, water, wine, bay leaves, oregano and rosemary. Bring to the boil, reduce heat to low, cover and simmer for 1 1/2 hours.
3. Remove lid from pan, simmer uncovered for another 1/2 hour, until gravy thickens. Combine lemon rind, parsley and garlic in a small bowl. Place Osso Bucco on serving plates and sprinkle with parsley mixture.
Fat per serve: 4 grams

> **HINT**
> This rich-tasting stew requires long, slow cooking but tastes even better reheated next day.

Osso Bucco (top) and Lamb with Red Capsicum Sauce

Beef Kebabs with Tomato Salsa

Preparation time:
15 minutes + standing + refrigeration
Total cooking time:
15 minutes
Serves 4

1 cup burghul
1 cup boiling water
400 g lean minced beef
1 cup chopped mint
1/2 cup chopped parsley
1 teaspoon ground cumin
8 wooden skewers

Tomato Salsa
1 large ripe tomato, finely chopped
1 red onion, finely chopped
2 tablespoons chopped fresh coriander
2–3 tablespoons lemon juice
1 teaspoon sugar
2 teaspoons grated lemon rind

1. Place burghul in pan, pour boiling water over, cover tightly. Leave for 15 minutes (all water should be absorbed).
2. Place beef, burghul, mint, parsley and cumin in processor; process until well mixed. Divide mixture into eight portions, mould each around a skewer. Refrigerate for at least 30 minutes.
3. Grill kebabs on a barbecue or under a preheated grill. Serve hot with salsa, salad and bread.
4. ***To make Tomato Salsa***: Combine all ingredients in a bowl. Mix well. Cover and refrigerate until needed.
Fat per serve: 5 grams

> HINT
> Some supermarkets sell very lean minced beef (often marked 95% fat-free). Or buy lean topside or rump steak, cut off all fat and mince in food processor.

Salmon Burgers

Preparation time:
20 minutes + 30 minutes refrigeration
Total cooking time:
10 minutes
Serves 6

1 cup cottage cheese
400 g can salmon, drained
1/2 cup wheatgerm
2 teaspoons finely grated lemon rind
1 small onion, finely chopped
1/4 cup chopped parsley
freshly ground black pepper
1 egg, lightly beaten

To serve:
6 flat bread rolls
4 lettuce leaves
1 large tomato, sliced
6 large slices canned beetroot, drained
1 cup bean sprouts
200 g non-fat yoghurt
1/4 cup chopped mint

1. Place cottage cheese in a sieve and press with the back of a spoon to drain off excess liquid.
2. Combine salmon, cottage cheese, wheatgerm, lemon rind, onion, parsley and pepper in a large mixing bowl. Add egg and stir until all ingredients are well combined.
3. Divide mixture into 6 equal portions and shape into burgers. Place burgers in a single layer on plates or a tray, cover with plastic wrap and refrigerate for 30 minutes.
4. Cook burgers in a non-stick frying pan for about 5 minutes on each side.
5. To serve, split rolls and toast under grill. Place lettuce leaf, tomato and beetroot on half of roll. Top with burger, bean sprouts, yoghurt, mint and top half of roll. Serve immediately.
Fat per serve: 7 grams

Beef Kebabs with Tomato Salsa (top) and Salmon Burgers

Desserts

These recipes use no fat. Most contain small amounts of either honey or sugar, but remember that too much of these foods will slow weight loss. Eat them in moderation, or save them for special occasions.

Sweet Vanilla Peaches

Preparation time:
5 minutes + several hours refrigeration
Total cooking time:
10 minutes
Serves 4

8 ripe peaches
3 cups white wine
2 tablespoons honey
1 vanilla bean, split lengthwise
mint leaves, to garnish

1. Place the peaches in a heatproof bowl. Cover with boiling water and leave for one minute; drain and remove skins—they will slip off easily.
2. Combine white wine, honey and vanilla bean in a large pan. Stir over low heat until honey has dissolved. Add peaches and poach until fruit is just tender. Remove from heat and allow to cool, then refrigerate for several hours. Remove vanilla bean, wash and store for re-use another time. Serve peaches simply in stemmed glasses with poaching liquid and a sprig of mint to garnish.
Fat per serve: 0 grams.

HINT
The sweet, white-fleshed peaches available in late summer are best for this recipe. In winter, try cooking peeled and cored pears in the same way and serve warm or chilled.

Sweet Vanilla Peaches (top) and Apricot Souffle

Apricot Souffle

Preparation time:
25 minutes
Total cooking time:
30 minutes
Serves 4

1 cup dried apricots (150 g), roughly chopped
1 cup orange juice
3 egg whites
2 tablespoons caster sugar
2 teaspoons icing sugar

1. Preheat oven to moderate 180°C. Brush four 1-cup capacity individual souffle dishes lightly with oil or melted butter. Sprinkle base and sides with caster sugar; shake off excess. Place a collar of baking paper around dishes, secure with string. Lightly grease the paper.
2. Place apricots and orange juice in medium pan, bring to boil, reduce heat and simmer until apricots are tender. Remove from heat and cool. Place in food processor and process until smooth.
3. Using electric beaters, beat egg whites in a small, dry bowl until soft peaks form. Add sugar gradually, beating well after each addition.
4. Using a large metal spoon, fold apricot puree through beaten egg white mixture. Spoon into prepared dishes and place dishes on a large oven tray. Bake for 20 minutes or until souffles are well risen and cooked through. Remove from oven, cut paper collars from dishes and serve immediately, sprinkled with sifted icing sugar.
Fat per serve: 0 grams.

Brandied Oranges

Preparation time:
15 minutes + 3 hours refrigeration
Total cooking time:
10 minutes
Serves 4

1 tablespoon finely shredded orange rind
1/2 cup water
1/2 cup sugar
6–8 oranges, peeled and all pith removed
1 cup orange juice
1/4 cup brandy

1. Place orange rind in small heatproof bowl, cover with boiling water and leave for 3–4 minutes; drain.
2. Combine water and sugar in small pan, stir until sugar dissolves; bring to boil. Add rind, cook 8–10 minutes or until rind is translucent (take care not to burn).
3. Cut oranges into slices and arrange in a glass bowl. Top with cooked rind and any remaining syrup. Combine juice and brandy, pour over oranges. Refrigerate at least 3 hours to allow flavours to blend. Serve very cold. Garnish with mint leaves, if desired.
Fat per serve: 0 grams.

Frozen Orange Mango Yoghurt

Preparation time:
10 minutes + freezing + refrigeration
Total cooking time:
Nil
Serves 6

2 mangoes
1/2 cup orange juice concentrate
1 kg no-fat natural yoghurt

Mango Sauce
2 mangoes
2 tablespoons lime juice

1. Peel mangoes, cut as much flesh off seeds as possible. Place flesh in food processor, add juice and yoghurt. Process until well combined. Pour into an ice-cream churn and freeze. If you don't have an ice-cream churn, pour into a cake tin and freeze until just firm around the edges. Remove from freezer

Brandied Oranges (left) and Frozen Orange Mango Yoghurt

and beat until smooth. Return to freezer until firm. Remove from freezer and place in refrigerator section 1 hour before serving. Serve scoops with Mango Sauce.

2. *To make Sauce:* Peel mangoes, cut as much flesh off seed as possible. In food processor or blender, combine mango with lime juice. Refrigerate until ready to serve.

Fat per serve: 0 grams.

Note: This will taste extra creamy made in an ice-cream churn. If you don't have one, freezing and beating by hand is worth the effort.

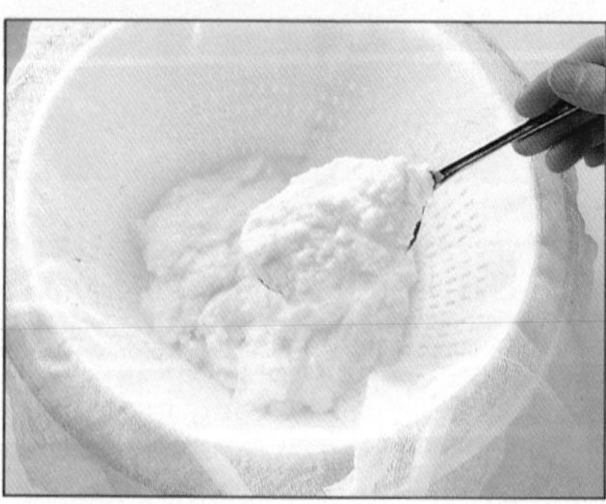

1 Spoon yoghurt into a muslin-lined strainer and leave to drain.

2 Place the rhubarb in a pan with the juice, honey, cinnamon stick and cloves.

Honey Rhubarb with Yoghurt

Preparation time:
10 minutes + 2 hours standing
Total cooking time:
8 minutes
Serves 4

500 g non-fat natural yoghurt
1 teaspoon vanilla essence
1 teaspoon finely grated orange rind
1 bunch rhubarb, washed and cut into 3 cm lengths
1/2 cup orange juice
2 tablespoons honey
1 cinnamon stick
6 whole cloves
1 teaspoon sugar
1 teaspoon ground cinnamon

1. Place yoghurt in medium bowl, add essence and rind and stir. Line a strainer with a piece of clean muslin (or a new Chux-style cloth) and pour in yoghurt. Leave to drain over a basin for at least 2 hours, preferably in the refrigerator.
2. Place rhubarb in a pan with juice, honey, cinnamon stick and cloves. Bring to the boil, cover and simmer over very low heat for 8 minutes. Remove from heat and leave to cool. Remove cinnamon stick and cloves and refrigerate rhubarb.
3. Combine sugar and ground cinnamon in a small bowl. Serve rhubarb topped with a dollop of drained yoghurt and sprinkled with sugar and cinnamon mixture. Serve chilled for best results. May be served hot in cold weather.
Fat per serve: 0 grams.

Honey Rhubarb with Yoghurt

3 Remove the cinnamon stick and cloves from the rhubarb mixture.

4 Combine the sugar and ground cinnamon in a small bowl.

Strawberry Yoghurt Ice-cream

Preparation time: 15 minutes + overnight freezing
Total cooking time: Nil
Serves 6

1 punnet strawberries, hulled (or use 300 g frozen blueberries or raspberries)
2 teaspoons gelatine
2 tablespoons orange juice
2 tablespoons honey
500 g non-fat natural yoghurt
2 egg whites
1 tablespoon sugar

1. Process berries in food processor until smooth. Combine gelatine and orange juice in a cup and place cup in a bowl of hot water (or microwave on High for 15 seconds); stir until gelatine dissolves.
2. Place honey and yoghurt in bowl; stir in gelatine mixture.
3. Beat egg whites until soft peaks form. Add sugar gradually, beating well after each addition until mixture is thick and glossy. Gently fold yoghurt and berry puree into beaten egg whites. Pour into a freezer container and freeze until just firm around edges. Remove from freezer, transfer to a large mixing bowl. Beat with electric beaters until creamy. Return to freezer, freeze overnight or until firm. Remove from freezer, place in refrigerator section 1 hour before serving to soften. Serve with fruit salad or berries.
Fat per serve: 0 grams.

Hot Winter Fruits

Preparation time: 10 minutes
Total cooking time: 15 minutes
Serves 4

12 dried apricots
12 prunes
1/2 cup raisins
1 cup orange juice
1 cinnamon stick
4 bananas, peeled and cut into chunks
1–2 tablespoons rum (or use extra orange juice)

1. In a pan, combine apricots, prunes, raisins, orange juice and cinnamon stick. Bring to boil, cover and simmer for 10 minutes.
2. Add bananas and continue cooking for 2–3 minutes. Add rum or extra juice and serve immediately. Fruits may also be served cold.
Fat per serve: 0 grams

Cinnamon Rice Pudding

Preparation time: 5 minutes
Total cooking time: 1 hour 20 minutes
Serves 4

1/2 cup short-grain rice
1 tablespoon sugar
2 tablespoons sultanas
1 teaspoon finely grated orange rind
3 cups skim milk
1/2 teaspoon ground cinnamon
2 teaspoons soft brown sugar

1. Brush a shallow 4-cup capacity heatproof dish lightly with oil or melted butter. Place rice in dish. Sprinkle with sugar, sultanas and orange rind. Pour milk over rice. Bake in slow150°C oven for 1 hour.
2. Combine cinnamon and brown sugar, sprinkle over pudding. Bake 20 minutes more. Serve pudding garnished with shredded orange rind, if desired.
Fat per serve: 0 grams.

Note: Add chopped dried apricots, if desired.

Hot Winter Fruits, Strawberry and Yoghurt Ice-cream and Cinnamon Rice Pudding

Index

Page numbers in italics refer to pictures

Front cover, clockwise from top left: Apricot Souffle (page 58), Seafood Hotpot (page 48) and Green Pea Soup (page 13)